IRISH
WIT &
WISDOM

Quips and Quotes to Suit
All Manner of Occasions

RICHARD BENSON

summersdale

IRISH WIT AND WISDOM

Summersdale Publishers Ltd
46 West Street
Chichester
West Sussex
PO19 1RP
UK

www.summersdale.com

Printed and bound in the Czech Republic

ISBN: 978-1-84953-846-6

Substantial discounts on bulk quantities of Summersdale books are available to corporations, professional associations and other organisations. For details contact Nicky Douglas by telephone: +44 (0) 1243 756902, fax: +44 (0) 1243 786300 or email: nicky@summersdale.com.

CONTENTS

EDITOR'S NOTE

The charm of Ireland and its remarkable people is, like the mythical Shannon that flows through many of its counties, seemingly endless. Irish history stretches back into the dark days of the Celts, yet there is light, laughter and a sense of laissez-faire in the Irish men and women of today. Few nations can claim to ridicule themselves so expertly as the Irish – the wicked wit of Oscar Wilde, for example, who claimed that 'Life is far too important a thing ever to talk seriously about', will live forever. James Joyce echoed this sentiment with his remark that 'Funerals in Ireland are so jolly they should be called funferalls.' Indeed, nothing in life seems to be able to dampen the enduring spirit of the Irish – though their history stretches back to the dark days of the Celts, they are, at the same time, 'ferociously tenacious', as Edna O'Brien put it. Where better to share a laugh than at the local tavern, where legendary Irish hospitality can be sampled? There you can toast, bless and curse your way through an evening, perhaps employing such classics as 'May all the goats in Gorey chase you to hell.'

These memorable sayings, and many more, can be found in this collection of Irish wit and wisdom.

CELTIC
CHARACTER

I'm a product of my Irish culture…
I could no more lose that than
I could my sense of identity.

GABRIEL BYRNE

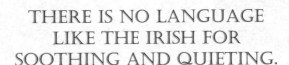

THERE IS NO LANGUAGE
LIKE THE IRISH FOR
SOOTHING AND QUIETING.

JOHN MILLINGTON SYNGE

The heart of an Irishman is
nothing but his imagination.

GEORGE BERNARD SHAW

EVERYONE IS A VISIONARY,
IF YOU SCRATCH HIM
DEEP ENOUGH. BUT
THE CELT, UNLIKE ANY
OTHER, IS A VISIONARY
WITHOUT SCRATCHING.

W. B. YEATS

All the world's a stage and most of
us are desperately unrehearsed.

SEÁN O'CASEY

I NEVER PUT OFF TILL
TOMORROW WHAT I CAN
POSSIBLY DO – THE DAY AFTER.

OSCAR WILDE

This is one race of people
for whom psychoanalysis is
of no use whatsoever.

SIGMUND FREUD

I'M IRISH.
WE THINK SIDEWAYS.

SPIKE MILLIGAN

Other people have a nationality.
The Irish… have a psychosis.

BRENDAN BEHAN

*The Irish do love
telling stories, and*

*we are suspicious of
people who don't have*

*long, complicated
conversations.*

MAEVE BINCHY

IT'S NOT THAT THE IRISH ARE
CYNICAL...RATHER THAT
THEY HAVE A WONDERFUL
LACK OF RESPECT FOR
EVERYTHING AND EVERYBODY.

BRENDAN BEHAN

Above all else, deep in my soul,
I'm a tough Irishwoman.

MAUREEN O'HARA

BEING IRISH IS VERY MUCH
A PART OF WHO I AM. I TAKE
IT EVERYWHERE WITH ME.

COLIN FARRELL

I can't think of anything you
might say about Irish people
that is absolutely true.

ANNE ENRIGHT

YOU CAN'T HEAR IRISH
TUNES WITHOUT KNOWING
YOU'RE IRISH, AND
WANTING TO POUND THAT
FACT INTO THE FLOOR.

JENNIFER ARMSTRONG

In Ireland most complaints
are made with a whisper.

DAVID MONAGAN

AN IRISHMAN WILL ALWAYS
SOFTEN BAD NEWS, SO THAT
A MAJOR CORONARY IS NO
MORE THAN 'A BAD TURN'.

HUGH LEONARD

If at first you don't succeed, try,
try again. Then quit… no point
in being a damn fool about it.

W. C. FIELDS

NO LIFE IS SO HARD THAT
YOU CAN'T MAKE IT EASIER
BY THE WAY YOU TAKE IT.

ELLEN GLASGOW

What do I know about man's destiny?
I could tell you more about radishes.

SAMUEL BECKETT

IRISH MALES ARE A PIECE OF WORK, ARE THEY NOT?

BONO

Overheard at O'Banion's Beer
Emporium: 'Pardon me, darlin',
but I'm writin' a telephone book.
C'n I have yer number?'

HENRY D. SPALDING

AH, IRELAND... THAT
DAMNABLE, DELIGHTFUL
COUNTRY, WHERE EVERYTHING
THAT IS RIGHT IS THE OPPOSITE
OF WHAT IT OUGHT TO BE.

BENJAMIN DISRAELI

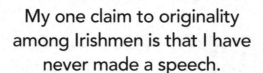

My one claim to originality
among Irishmen is that I have
never made a speech.

GEORGE MOORE

WHEN I DIE DUBLIN
WILL BE WRITTEN
IN MY HEART.

JAMES JOYCE

Ireland is where strange tales begin
and happy endings are possible.

CHARLES HAUGHEY

IN IRELAND THE INEVITABLE
NEVER HAPPENS AND
THE UNEXPECTED
CONSTANTLY OCCURS.

JOHN PENTLAND MAHAFFY

When anyone asks me about the
Irish character, I say look at the
trees. Maimed, stark and misshapen,
but ferociously tenacious.

EDNA O'BRIEN

LOVE IS NEVER DEFEATED. AND,
I COULD ADD, THE HISTORY
OF IRELAND PROVES THAT, IF
IT WERE NOT SO, HUMANITY
WOULD ONLY BE CONDEMNED
TO DESTRUCTION.

POPE JOHN PAUL II

Listen to our tunes, observe
a Celtic scroll: we always
decorate our essence.

FRANK DELANEY

THE IRISH SEEM TO HAVE
MORE FIRE ABOUT THEM
THAN THE SCOTS.

SEAN CONNERY

My dad was a really silly man. A
great Irish silly man. And that's fine.

JOAN CUSACK

IF YOU'RE FORTUNATE... YOU
COME FROM THE KIDDING
KIND OF IRISH FAMILY.

P. J. O'ROURKE

THE
EMERALD
ISLE

There's no need to fear the wind
if your haystacks are tied down.

IRISH PROVERB

THE INNER CITY
ARCHITECTURE OF DUBLIN IS
LIKE A LADY IN THE MORNING
WITHOUT HER MAKE-UP ON.

JIM TUNNEY

I went to Ireland once… it was a
beautiful country, and both the
women and men were good-looking.

JAMES CAGNEY

EVERY CRAG AND
GNARLED TREE AND
LONELY VALLEY HAS
ITS OWN STRANGE AND
GRACEFUL LEGEND
ATTACHED TO IT.

Douglas Hyde

Ireland's ruins are historic
emotions surrendered to time.

HORACE SUTTON

NOW SWEETLY LIES
OLD IRELAND
EMERALD GREEN
BEYOND THE FOAM,
AWAKENING SWEET MEMORIES,
CALLING THE HEART
BACK HOME.

ANONYMOUS

This little country that inspires
the biggest things – your
best days are still ahead.

BARACK OBAMA, ON IRELAND

O, IRELAND! ISN'T
GRAND YOU LOOK—
LIKE A BRIDE IN HER
RICH ADORNIN!
WITH ALL THE PENT-UP
LOVE OF MY HEART
I BID YOU THE TOP OF
THE MORNING!

JOHN LOCKE

Capital punishment means
having to live in Ireland.

SEAN KILROY

TO ANYONE WITH A DROP
OF IRISH BLOOD IN THEM
THE LAND THEY LIVE ON
IS LIKE THEIR MOTHER.

ALEXANDRA RIPLEY

Ireland, in breadth, and for
wholesomeness and serenity
of climate, far surpasses Britain.

VENERABLE BEDE

WE HAVE THE SOULS OF POETS...
WE DELIGHT IN THE BEAUTY
OF STRANGE PLACES AND
DARK PLACES IN OUR HEARTS.

EILIS FLYNN

Geographically, Ireland is a
medium-sized rural island that
is slowly but steadily being
consumed by sheep.

DAVE BARRY

LAUGH

IT

OFF

Why should you never
iron a four-leaf clover?

You don't want
to press your luck.

DARYL STOUT

THE ONE THING US IRISH HAVE
IS THE ABILITY TO LAUGH AT
OURSELVES... GOD BLESS US ALL.

ANN KENNEDY

They treat a joke as a serious thing
and a serious thing as a joke.

SEÁN O'CASEY

I'M IRISH, SO I'M MESSING
ALL THE TIME. WHICH MEANS,
I'M HAVING A LAUGH. I'M
ALWAYS MAKING JOKES.

SAOIRSE RONAN

The Irish and British, they love satire,
it's a large part of the culture.

BEN NICHOLSON

NOTHING IS AS EASY AS IT
LOOKS; EVERYTHING TAKES
LONGER THAN YOU EXPECT;
AND IF ANYTHING CAN GO
WRONG, IT WILL AND AT THE
WORST POSSIBLE MOMENT.

MURPHY'S LAW

Everyone is wise until he speaks.

IRISH PROVERB

THE IRISH IGNORE ANYTHING THEY CAN'T DRINK OR PUNCH.

IRISH PROVERB

A quiet Irishman is about as harmless as a powder magazine built over a match factory.

JAMES DUNNE

THE IRISH GAVE THE BAGPIPES TO THE SCOTS AS A JOKE, BUT THE SCOTS HAVEN'T SEEN THE JOKE YET.

OLIVER HERFORD

You're not too old when
your hair turns grey.
You're not too old when
your teeth decay.
But you'll know you're
awaiting that final sleep,
When your mind makes promises
your body can't keep.

ANONYMOUS

IF IT WAS RAINING SOUP, THE IRISH WOULD GO OUT WITH FORKS.

BRENDAN BEHAN

A good laugh and a long sleep are
the two best cures for anything.

IRISH PROVERB

IRISH ALZHEIMER'S:
YOU FORGET
EVERYTHING EXCEPT
THE GRUDGES.

Judy Collins

AN IRISHMAN WAS ASKED
IF THE IRISH ALWAYS
ANSWER ONE QUESTION
WITH ANOTHER. 'WHO TOLD
YOU THAT?' HE REPLIED.

NIALL TÓIBÍN

Here's to eyes in your heads
and none in your spuds.

IRISH TOAST

CONTRACEPTIVES SHOULD
BE USED ON EVERY
CONCEIVABLE OCCASION.

SPIKE MILLIGAN

One swallow doesn't
make a pint.

RICHARD HARRIS

OF THEIR QUICKNESS
AS TO THE HUMOUR
THERE CAN BE NO DOUBT.

**CHARLES DICKENS
ON HIS DUBLIN AUDIENCE**

Everyone is nice

until the cow gets
into the garden.

IRISH PROVERB

Is it still considered a shock if you
intentionally touch an electric fence?

MARK O'DOHERTY

EVERYTHING IS FUNNY
AS LONG AS IT IS HAPPENING
TO SOMEONE ELSE.

WILL ROGERS

My way of joking is to tell the truth.
It's the funniest joke in the world.

GEORGE BERNARD SHAW

IN IRELAND EVERYBODY IN
THE ROOM ALREADY THINKS
THEY'RE FUNNY, SO YOU'VE
GOT TO PROVE TO THEM
THAT YOU'RE FUNNIER.

JASON BYRNE

If you want to tell people
the truth, make them laugh,
otherwise they'll kill you.

OSCAR WILDE

IF YOU'VE GOT NOTHING
BUT A SENSE OF HUMOUR,
YOU WILL SURVIVE.

PHIL LYNOTT

DRINK
UP

Ireland sober is Ireland stiff.

JAMES JOYCE

MAY THE JOYS OF TODAY
BE THOSE OF TOMORROW.
THE GOBLETS OF LIFE
HOLD NO DREGS OF SORROW.

IRISH TOAST

I know I've got Irish blood
because I wake up every
day with a… hangover.

NOEL GALLAGHER

WHEN WE DRINK,
WE GET DRUNK.
WHEN WE GET DRUNK,
WE FALL ASLEEP.
WHEN WE FALL ASLEEP,
WE COMMIT NO SIN.
WHEN WE COMMIT NO
SIN, WE GO TO HEAVEN.
SOOOOO, LET'S ALL GET
DRUNK, AND GO TO HEAVEN!

IRISH TOAST

Only Irish coffee provides in a single
glass all four essential food groups:
alcohol, caffeine, sugar and fat.

ALEX LEVINE

**THE PROBLEM WITH
SOME PEOPLE IS THAT
WHEN THEY AREN'T
DRUNK, THEY'RE SOBER.**

W. B. Yeats

THOSE WHO DRINK TO FORGET, PLEASE PAY IN ADVANCE.

SIGN AT THE HIBERNIAN BAR, CORK CITY

The drink and I have been friends for so long, it would be a pity for me to leave without one last kiss.

TURLOUGH O'CAROLAN

MAY THE WINDS OF FORTUNE SAIL YOU, MAY YOU SAIL A GENTLE SEA. MAY IT ALWAYS BE THE OTHER GUY WHO SAYS, 'THIS DRINK'S ON ME.'

IRISH TOAST

May you have the health
of a salmon – a strong
heart and a wet mouth.

IRISH TOAST

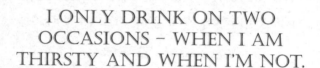

I ONLY DRINK ON TWO
OCCASIONS – WHEN I AM
THIRSTY AND WHEN I'M NOT.

BRENDAN BEHAN

I'm Irish and the Irish are
very emotionally moved. My
mother is Irish and she cries
during beer commercials.

BARRY McCAFFREY

GOD INVENTED WHISKEY
SO THE IRISH WOULDN'T
RULE THE WORLD.

ANONYMOUS

Love may make the world go
round, but not as fast as whiskey.

RICHARD HARRIS

MAY YOU ALWAYS HAVE
A CLEAN SHIRT, A CLEAR
CONSCIENCE, AND ENOUGH
COINS IN YOUR POCKET
TO BUY A PINT!

IRISH TOAST

Ireland is the only country in the world where there are protestors outside AA meetings.

DES BISHOP

OH, HE OCCASIONALLY TAKES AN ALCOHOLIDAY.

OSCAR WILDE TALKING ABOUT HIS BROTHER

I drink therefore I am.
I'm drunk therefore I was.

SEAMUS O'LEARY

What whiskey will not cure, there is no cure for.

IRISH PROVERB

MANY PEOPLE DIE OF
THIRST BUT THE IRISH
ARE BORN WITH ONE.

SPIKE MILLIGAN

Work is the curse
of the drinking classes.

OSCAR WILDE

ALL YOU
CAN EAT

I finally found a diet that works in Ireland. I only eat when the weather's good.

HAL ROACH

I'M IRISH, SO I'M USED TO ODD STEWS.

LIAM NEESON

A turkey never voted for
an early Christmas.

IRISH PROVERB

THERE IS NO LOVE SINCERER
THAN THE LOVE OF FOOD.

GEORGE BERNARD SHAW

He was a bold man that
first ate an oyster.

JONATHAN SWIFT

LAUGHTER IS BRIGHTEST WHERE FOOD IS BEST.

Irish proverb

MAY YOU HAVE FOOD
AND RAIMENT,
A SOFT PILLOW FOR
YOUR HEAD,
MAY YOU BE FORTY
YEARS IN HEAVEN
BEFORE THE DEVIL
KNOWS YOU'RE DEAD.

IRISH BLESSING

I want my food dead.
Not sick, not dying, dead.

OSCAR WILDE

SPORTING

AMBITIONS

I ASKED HER FOR A PINT OF HARP AND A PACKET OF CRISPS.

STEPHEN FERRIS ON MEETING THE QUEEN

It's always nice to start off with a good result.

ROBBIE KEANE

A CLAP ON THE BACK IS ONLY ABOUT TWO FEET FROM A KICK IN THE ARSE.

BABS KEATING

Whenever a team loses, there's always a row at half time but when they win, it's an inspirational speech.

JOHN O'MAHONY

ONE THING I LEARNT EARLY ON MY CAREER IS THAT PERSONAL GRATIFICATION TAKES SECOND PLACE.

BRIAN O'DRISCOLL

You need dictatorships and poverty to produce great footballers.

EAMON DUNPHY

A NEWSPAPER HEADLINE
YOU'LL NEVER GET TO SEE:
'POLICE WARN OF TROUBLE
FROM GOLF HOOLIGANS.'

ROBERT O'BYRNE

I gave up shadow-boxing the
night my shadow beat me up.

JAMES McKEON

THEY HAVE A FORWARD LINE
THAT COULDN'T PUNCH
HOLES IN A PAPER BAG.

PAT SPILLANE ON THE CAVAN TEAM

He's got a knock on his shin
there, just above the knee.

FRANK STAPLETON

IT WASN'T A MONKEY
ON MY BACK, IT WAS
PLANET OF THE APES.

MICK McCARTHY

In golf… if you dress
the part people believe
you can actually play.

EAMONN HOLMES

NEVER TAKE YOUR EYES OFF
THE BALL – EVEN WHEN IT'S
IN THE REFEREE'S POCKET.

CHRISTY RING

Life isn't all beer and football…
some of us haven't touched
a football in months.

**A KERRY PLAYER DURING
1980s LEAGUE CAMPAIGN**

YOU GET MORE CONTACT IN
AN OLD-TIME WALTZ AT THE
OLD-FOLKS' HOME THAN IN
A NATIONAL LEAGUE FINAL.

PAT SPILLANE

I want a quick, skilful and athletic team.

I'd rather have greyhounds than elephants.

JIMMY BARRY-MURPHY

Football is a game for those not good enough to play hurling.

TONY WALL

A KERRY FOOTBALLER WITH AN INFERIORITY COMPLEX IS ONE WHO THINKS HE'S JUST AS GOOD AS EVERYBODY ELSE.

JOHN B. KEANE

My idea of exercising is striking a match for a cigarette.

ANNE MARIE SCANLON

OLLIE MURPHY IS AFTER
THROWING SO MANY
DUMMIES, YOU WOULDN'T
SEE THE LIKES IN A CRÈCHE.

KEVIN MALLON

A golf club is a stick with a head
on one end and a fool on the other.

DAMIEN MULDOON

ANY CHANCE OF
AN AUTOGRAPH?
IT'S FOR THE WIFE...
SHE REALLY HATES YOU.

TIPP FAN TO GER LOUGHNANE

GOOD FOR THE
CONSTITUTION

He knows nothing; and he thinks
he knows everything. That points
clearly to a political career.

GEORGE BERNARD SHAW

THE WORST THREAT TO
IRISH FARMERS IS NOT
FOOT-AND-MOUTH DISEASE,
BUT A POSTAL STRIKE.

RURAL IRISH PROVERB

The weak are a
long time in politics.

NEIL SHAND

IRELAND HAS THE BEST
POLITICIANS MONEY
CAN BUY.

SAM SNORT

I solemnly swear that this
oath is not an oath.

DAN BREEN

WE SHOULD SILENCE ANYONE
WHO OPPOSES THE RIGHT
TO FREEDOM OF SPEECH.

BOYLE ROCHE

Any political party
that includes the word
'democratic' in its name, isn't.

PATRICK MURRAY

THE MAIN QUALIFICATION
FOR BEING A ROYAL IS TO
SMILE CONSTANTLY AND
PRETEND YOU'RE HAVING A
GREAT TIME EVERYWHERE.

MAEVE BINCHY

The minority is sometimes right;
the majority always wrong.

GEORGE BERNARD SHAW

I DON'T LIKE POLITICAL
JOKES. TOO MANY OF
THEM GET ELECTED.

DONAL FOLEY

A man should always be
drunk… when he talks politics
– it's the only way in which
to make them important.

SEÁN O'CASEY

NOTHING IS POLITICALLY RIGHT WHICH IS MORALLY WRONG.

DANIEL O'CONNELL

To gain that which is worth having, it may be necessary to lose everything else.

BERNADETTE DEVLIN

THE VOTE... MEANS NOTHING TO WOMEN, WE SHOULD BE ARMED.

EDNA O'BRIEN

My electioneering style? I
kiss the mothers and shake
hands with the babies.

JOE COSTELLO

WHY DO YOU STAND FOR
ELECTION TO GET A SEAT?

DONAL FOLEY

The art of government is the
organisation of idolatry.

GEORGE BERNARD SHAW

IRELAND VS
THE WORLD

I HAD TO HAVE SOME BALLS
TO BE IRISH CATHOLIC IN
SOUTH LONDON. MOST OF
THAT TIME I SPENT FIGHTING.

PIERCE BROSNAN

The Irish remember too much
and the English too little.

EILIS O'HANLON

WE HAVE ALWAYS FOUND
THE IRISH A BIT ODD.
THEY REFUSE TO BE ENGLISH.

WINSTON CHURCHILL

Hebrews and Gaels have much in common. Both are exotic enough to be interesting and not foreign enough to be alarming.

BRENDAN BEHAN

THE ENGLISH ARE NOT HAPPY UNLESS THEY ARE MISERABLE, THE IRISH ARE NOT AT PEACE UNLESS THEY ARE AT WAR.

GEORGE ORWELL

The problem with Ireland is that it's a country full of genius, but with absolutely no talent.

HUGH LEONARD

MY PASSPORT'S GREEN.

SEAMUS HEANEY

Americans… will go on adoring me until I say something nice about them.

GEORGE BERNARD SHAW

YOU THINK THE WELSH
ARE FRIENDLY, BUT THE
IRISH ARE FABULOUS.

BONNIE TYLER

The Irish seem to have more fire
about them than the Scots.

SEAN CONNERY

NATIONS HAVE THEIR EGO,
JUST LIKE INDIVIDUALS.

JAMES JOYCE

THERE ARE ONLY TWO
KINDS OF PEOPLE
IN THE WORLD, THE
IRISH AND THOSE WHO
WISH THEY WERE.

Anonymous

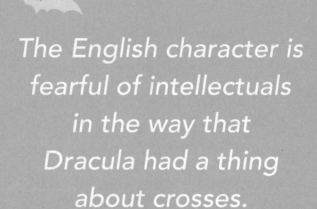

The English character is fearful of intellectuals in the way that Dracula had a thing about crosses.

DECLAN LYNCH

FOR MANY YEARS I THOUGHT
AN INNUENDO WAS AN
ITALIAN SUPPOSITORY.

SPIKE MILLIGAN

A Mexican straight flush
is any five cards and a gun.

HUGH LEONARD

ONE ALWAYS LOVES THE
COUNTRY ONE HAS
CONQUERED, AND I HAVE
CONQUERED ENGLAND.

GEORGE BERNARD SHAW

We don't have anything as
urgent as mañana in Ireland.

STUART BANKS

UNDER THE ENGLISH
LEGAL SYSTEM YOU ARE
INNOCENT UNTIL YOU
ARE SHOWN TO BE IRISH.

TED WHITEHEAD

The reason the Irish are always
fighting each other is they have
no other worthy opponents.

ANONYMOUS

DIVINE
INTERVENTION

I suffer from Irish-Catholic guilt.

EDWARD BURNS

WE HAVE JUST ENOUGH
RELIGION TO MAKE US HATE,
BUT NOT ENOUGH TO MAKE
US LOVE ONE ANOTHER.

JONATHAN SWIFT

God's help is nearer than the door.

IRISH PROVERB

I'M AN ATHEIST... THANK GOD.

DAVE ALLEN

Irish atheists have started a
'Dial-A-Prayer' service. When you
phone them up, nobody answers.

HAL ROACH

I'M A BAD CATHOLIC.
IT'S THE RELIGION OF
ALL GREAT ARTISTS.

BRENDAN BEHAN

God is good, but never
dance in a small boat.

IRISH PROVERB

I'M AN IRISH CATHOLIC
AND I HAVE A LONG
ICEBERG OF GUILT.

EDNA O'BRIEN

St Patrick brought Christianity
to Ireland. It's a pity the
idea never caught on.

GEORGE BERNARD SHAW

I'm terrified about the day that
I enter the gates of heaven and
God says to me, 'Just a minute.'

MAUREEN O'HARA

BUT LET'S JUST SAY,
I'M IRISH. I GREW UP IN
THE 1950s. RELIGION HAD
A VERY TIGHT IRON FIST.

LIAM NEESON

WHAT THEY DO IN
HEAVEN WE ARE
IGNORANT OF; WHAT
THEY DO NOT WE ARE
TOLD EXPRESSLY.

Jonathan Swift

The great Gaels of Ireland are
the men that God made mad,
For all their wars are merry,
and all their songs are sad.

G. K. CHESTERTON

THE LESS YOU KNOW, THE MORE YOU BELIEVE.

BONO

Love all men – except lawyers.

IRISH PROVERB

WHEN GOD MADE TIME,
HE MADE PLENTY OF IT.

IRISH PROVERB

God did not intend for
Irish kids to play in the sun,
according to my mother.

LAURIE HALSE ANDERSON

ALL THE THINGS WE LOATHE
IN HUMAN BEINGS ARE THE
ATTRIBUTES WE GIVE TO... GOD.

DAVID FEHERTY

When did I realise I was God?
Well, I was praying and I suddenly
realised I was talking to myself.

PETER O'TOOLE

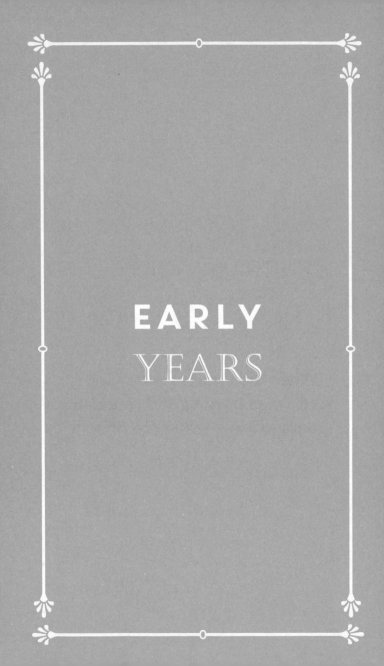

EARLY

YEARS

YOUTH IS A WONDERFUL
THING. WHAT A CRIME TO
WASTE IT ON CHILDREN.

GEORGE BERNARD SHAW

You've got to do your own
growing, no matter how tall
your grandfather was.

IRISH PROVERB

NO MAN IS RICH ENOUGH
TO BUY BACK HIS PAST.

OSCAR WILDE

Age is honourable
and youth is noble.

IRISH PROVERB

THE FIRST TWO-SYLLABLE
WORD I EVER LEARNED
GROWING UP WAS
'DISCRETION'.

EAMON DUNPHY

I was a slow developer.
I didn't develop my first
birthmark until I was five.

JAMES McKEON

I really did look like a baked bean until I was thirteen.

BONO

YOU CANNOT PUT AN OLD HEAD ON THE YOUNG.

Irish proverb

THE OLD BELIEVE EVERYTHING;
THE MIDDLE-AGED SUSPECT
EVERYTHING; THE YOUNG
KNOW EVERYTHING.

OSCAR WILDE

Youth does not mind
where it sets its foot.

IRISH PROVERB

I HAVE THE BODY OF AN
EIGHTEEN YEAR OLD.
I KEEP IT IN THE FRIDGE.

SPIKE MILLIGAN

Young people don't know what old age is, and old people forget what youth was.

IRISH PROVERB

I HAD A VERY HAPPY CHILDHOOD, WHICH IS UNSUITABLE IF YOU'RE GOING TO BE AN IRISH WRITER.

MAEVE BINCHY

It's all that the young can do for the old, to shock them and keep them up to date.

GEORGE BERNARD SHAW

THE ARROGANCE OF
AGE MUST SUBMIT TO BE
TAUGHT BY YOUTH.

EDMUND BURKE

I first gave up smoking
when I was eight.

DAVE ALLEN

I WAS THE SEVENTH OF
NINE CHILDREN. WHEN
YOU COME FROM THAT
FAR DOWN YOU HAVE TO
STRUGGLE TO SURVIVE.

ROBERT F. KENNEDY

AGE IS JUST
A NUMBER

You know you're growing old
when the light of your life
is the one in the fridge.

HAL ROACH

WE'RE NOT THE MEN OUR
FATHERS WERE. IF WE WERE
WE'D BE TERRIBLY OLD.

FLANN O'BRIEN

No woman should ever be
quite accurate about her age.
It looks so calculating.

OSCAR WILDE

HE WAS AT DEATH'S
DOOR, BUT THE DOCTOR
PULLED HIM THROUGH.

FRANK CARSON

If I don't die in autumn I always
seem to survive until Christmas.

RICHARD BRINSLEY SHERIDAN

Never worry
about your
heart

till it stops
beating.

E. B. WHITE

PRAISE YOUTH AND IT WILL PROSPER.

Irish proverb

An aged man is but a paltry thing,
A tattered coat upon a stick.

W. B. YEATS

THERE'S NO POINT TAKING
OUT LIFE INSURANCE.
MY UNCLE DID AND
HE DIED ALL THE SAME.

SEAN KILROY

Young men want to be faithful,
and are not; old men want to
be faithless, and cannot.

OSCAR WILDE

IT'S THE BEST DAY OF
YOUR LIFE. YOU'VE PAID
FOR EVERYTHING AND
YOU CAN'T JOIN IN.

DAVE ALLEN ON AN IRISH WAKE

I can be eccentric now
and get away with it.

RICHARD HARRIS ON TURNING 70

AT A CERTAIN AGE SOME PEOPLE'S MINDS CLOSE UP; THEY LIVE ON THEIR INTELLECTUAL FAT.

IRISH PROVERB

The only exercise I take is walking behind the coffins of friends who took exercise.

PETER O'TOOLE

I DON'T ACTUALLY THINK YOU BECOME WISER, YOU JUST GET MORE EXPERIENCED.

PHIL LYNOTT

CAMARADERIE

There are no strangers here;
only friends you haven't yet met.

W. B. YEATS

TRUE FRIENDS STAB
YOU IN THE FRONT.

OSCAR WILDE

I am accusing him of stealing my best
material, he was a very funny man.

FRANK CARSON ON A FELLOW COMEDIAN

MAY THE HINGES
OF OUR FRIENDSHIP
NEVER GROW RUSTY.

IRISH TOAST

If you're Irish, it doesn't matter
where you go – you'll find family.

VICTORIA SMURFIT

*A secret in Dublin
means just telling
one person at
a time.*

**CIARÁN
MacGONIGAL**

LAUGHTER IS NOT AT ALL
A BAD BEGINNING FOR A
FRIENDSHIP, AND IT IS FAR
THE BEST ENDING FOR ONE.

OSCAR WILDE

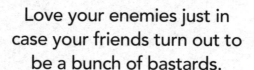

Love your enemies just in
case your friends turn out to
be a bunch of bastards.

R. A. DICKSON

The Irish are a fair people;
they never speak well
of one another.

SAMUEL JOHNSON

MAY FRIENDSHIP, LIKE WINE,
IMPROVE AS TIME ADVANCES.
AND MAY WE ALWAYS HAVE
OLD WINE, OLD FRIENDS
AND YOUNG CARES.

IRISH TOAST

A true friend never gets in your
way unless you happen
to be going down.

ARNOLD H. GLASOW

A FRIEND'S EYE IS
A GOOD MIRROR.

Irish proverb

FRIENDSHIP WILL NOT STAND
THE STRAIN OF VERY MUCH
GOOD ADVICE FOR VERY LONG.

ROBERT LYND

May you taste the sweetest pleasures
that fortune ere bestowed, and
may all your friends remember
all the favours you are owed.

IRISH TOAST

DUBLIN IS A CITY WHERE
THERE'S FAMILIARITY
WITHOUT FRIENDSHIP,
LONELINESS WITHOUT
SOLITUDE.

BRENDAN BEHAN

WHEN OF A GOSSIPING CIRCLE IT WAS ASKED, 'WHAT ARE THEY DOING?' THE ANSWER WAS, 'SWAPPING LIES.'

RICHARD BRINSLEY SHERIDAN

Anywhere you go liking everyone, everyone will be likeable.

MIGNON McLAUGHLIN

MUSICAL
NOTES

A lament in one ear, maybe,
but always a song in the other.

SEÁN O'CASEY

MAYBE IT'S BRED IN THE BONE,
BUT THE SOUND OF PIPES IS
A LITTLE BIT OF HEAVEN.

NANCY O'KEEFE

If there's music in hell,
it'll be the bagpipes.

JOE TOMELTY

NOBODY WANTS TO HEAR METALLICA AT LUNCHTIME.

MICHAEL FASSBENDER

If you've nothing to say, that's the first line of the song: 'I've nothing to say.'

BONO

I'M LOOKING FOR COMPENSATION FOR PSYCHOLOGICAL STRESS CAUSED BY THE BARBRA STREISAND CONCERT. I COULD HEAR HER SINGING.

SHANE HORGAN

He was a fiddler,
and consequently a rogue.

JONATHAN SWIFT

THE PROBLEM WITH
BEING IRISH... IS HAVING
'RIVERDANCE' ON YOUR BACK.
IT'S A BURDEN AT TIMES.

RODDY DOYLE

May the sound of happy music
and the lilt of irish laughter fill
your heart with gladness.

IRISH BLESSING

I LOVE THE MYSTERY AND THE LEGEND OF THE IRISH MUSIC.

MARY LESTER

Ronan Keating wants to be Robbie Williams, but what he really is is Cliff Richard.

LOUIS WALSH

PEOPLE FORGET THAT WHEN ELVIS WAS ALIVE, YOU COULDN'T GIVE HIS RECORDS AWAY.

MICHAEL O'RIORDAN

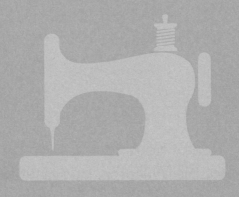

*I come from
a family of musicians.
Even the sewing
machine is a Singer.*

FRANK CARSON

People young and old come to listen to the traditional Irish music. Everyone's welcome. Everyone is Irish for the day.

MIKE SAFFRAN

SITTING IN THE WEST OF IRELAND, DOWNING YOUR THIRD PINT OF GUINNESS AND KNOWING IT'S GREAT TO BE IRISH.

CONOR CUNNEEN ON THE BEST WAY TO LISTEN TO IRISH MUSIC

Music can change the world because it can change people.

BONO

SLEEP IS AN EXCELLENT WAY
OF LISTENING TO AN OPERA.

JAMES STEPHENS

His vibrato sounded like he was
driving a tractor over ploughed fields
with weights tied to his scrotum.

SPIKE MILLIGAN

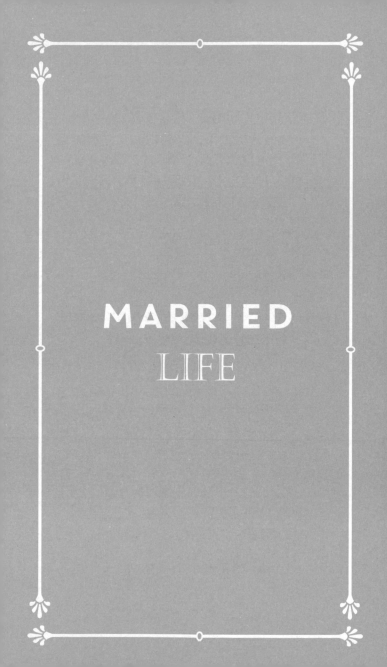

MARRIED
LIFE

IRISH WOMEN ARE ALWAYS
CARRYING WATER ON
THEIR HEADS, AND ALWAYS
CARRYING THEIR HUSBANDS
HOME FROM PUBS.

PETER O'TOOLE

Here's to our wives and girlfriends:
May they never meet!

IRISH TOAST

THE FICKLENESS OF THE
WOMEN I LOVE IS ONLY
EQUALLED BY THE INFERNAL
CONSTANCY OF THE
WOMEN WHO LOVE ME.

GEORGE BERNARD SHAW

When you marry your mistress,
you create a job vacancy.

JAMES GOLDSMITH

IT WAS A PERFECT MARRIAGE.
SHE DIDN'T WANT TO
AND HE COULDN'T.

SPIKE MILLIGAN

I am married to a very
dear girl who is an artist.
We have no children except me.

BRENDAN BEHAN

SHE WATCHES HIM AS A
CAT WOULD WATCH
A MOUSE.

JONATHAN SWIFT ON IRISH WIVES

IRISH WOMEN LIKE THE SIMPLE THINGS IN LIFE – LIKE IRISH MEN.

MARY COUGHLAN

I once knew a guy who thought 'loading the dishwasher' meant getting his wife drunk.

SIL FOX

Virtue in a man doesn't make
you want to grab him.

CAITLIN THOMAS

YOU CAN'T KISS AN
IRISH GIRL UNEXPECTEDLY.
YOU CAN ONLY KISS
HER SOONER THAN SHE
THOUGHT YOU WOULD.

IRISH PROVERB

The ideal wife for an Irishman is a
rich dumb blonde nymphomaniac
who owns a pub near a racecourse.

SEAN KILROY

Foreplay, in Ireland,
is the technical term for
taking your shoes off.

JOSEPH O'CONNOR

IF A MAN BUYS HIS GIRLFRIEND
A SEE-THROUGH DRESS, HIS
MOTIVES ARE TRANSPARENT.

SINÉAD CUSACK

I'm giving up marriage for Lent.

BRIAN BEHAN

MEN ALWAYS WANT TO BE
A WOMAN'S FIRST LOVE
– WOMEN LIKE TO BE A
MAN'S LAST ROMANCE.

OSCAR WILDE

There are only three kinds of
Irish men who can't understand
women – young men, old men,
and men of middle age.

IRISH PROVERB

I DON'T TELL MY WIFE
ANYTHING. I FIGURE
THAT WHAT SHE DOESN'T
KNOW WON'T HURT ME.

DANNY CUMMINS

WHAT'S THE
CRAIC?

Whenever something negative happens, there is always somebody quick with a smart remark to relax the mood.

CECILIA AHERN

LIFE IS FAR TOO IMPORTANT A THING EVER TO TALK SERIOUSLY ABOUT IT.

OSCAR WILDE

If you're enough lucky to be Irish… you're lucky enough!

IRISH PROVERB

MAY YOUR HEART BE
WARM AND HAPPY
WITH THE LILT OF
IRISH LAUGHTER
EVERY DAY IN EVERY WAY
AND FOREVER AND
EVER AFTER.

IRISH TOAST

Even when they have nothing,
the Irish emit a kind of
happiness, a joy.

FIONA SHAW

A GOOD LAUGH AND
A LONG SLEEP ARE
THE TWO BEST CURES.

Irish proverb

IT'S MY RULE NEVER TO LOSE ME TEMPER TILL IT WOULD BE DETRIMENTAL TO KEEP IT.

SEÁN O'CASEY

Nothing is funnier than unhappiness, I grant you that... Yes, yes, it's the most comical thing in the world.

SAMUEL BECKETT

HAPPINESS CAN'T BUY MONEY.

MAUREEN POTTER

Funerals in Ireland are so jolly
they should be called funferalls.

JAMES JOYCE

ONE OF THE BEST LESSONS
YOU CAN LEARN IN
LIFE IS TO MASTER HOW
TO REMAIN CALM.

CATHERINE PULSIFER

If you make up your mind not to be
happy there's no reason why you
shouldn't have a fairly good time.

EDITH WHARTON

ANGER WITH STUPIDITY
IS THE MOST EXHAUSTING
OF EMOTIONS.

W. B. YEATS

Bless your little Irish heart
and every other Irish part.

IRISH BLESSING

THERE IS ALWAYS SOMETHING
RIDICULOUS ABOUT THE
EMOTIONS OF PEOPLE WHOM
ONE HAS CEASED TO LOVE.

OSCAR WILDE

You've got to play the hand that you're dealt and stop wishing for another hand.

MAEVE BINCHY

May your thoughts be as
glad as the shamrocks.
May your heart be as light as a song.
May each day bring you
bright happy hours,
That stay with you all year long.

IRISH BLESSING

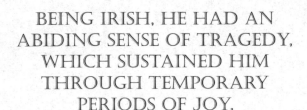

BEING IRISH, HE HAD AN
ABIDING SENSE OF TRAGEDY,
WHICH SUSTAINED HIM
THROUGH TEMPORARY
PERIODS OF JOY.

ANONYMOUS

THE
ENEMY

Always forgive your enemies;
nothing annoys them so much.

OSCAR WILDE

THE IRISH DO NOT WANT
ANYONE TO WISH THEM WELL;
THEY WANT EVERYONE TO
WISH THEIR ENEMIES ILL.

HAROLD NICOLSON

A quarrel is like buttermilk:
once it's out of the churn,
the more you shake it,
the more sour it grows.

IRISH PROVERB

MAY THE ENEMIES OF IRELAND
NEVER MEET A FRIEND.

IRISH CURSE

I learned long ago,
never to wrestle with
a pig. You get dirty,
and besides, the pig likes it.

GEORGE BERNARD SHAW

DON'T GO TO BED MAD.
STAY UP AND PLOT
YOUR REVENGE.

PAUL CASEY

NEVER HIT A MAN
WITH GLASSES.
USE A BRICK.

Seamus O'Leary

Money couldn't buy friends,
but you got a better
class of enemy.

SPIKE MILLIGAN

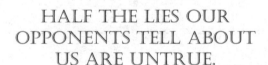

HALF THE LIES OUR
OPPONENTS TELL ABOUT
US ARE UNTRUE.

BOYLE ROCHE

Better be quarrelling
than lonesome.

IRISH PROVERB

Ireland is a peaceful country
and we'll fight anyone
who says otherwise.

RICHARD O'CONNOR

NEVER SPEAK WHEN YOU ARE
ANGRY. IF YOU DO YOU'LL
MAKE THE BEST SPEECH
YOU'LL EVER REGRET.

ROBERT LYND

THE MAN WHO SMILES WHEN
THINGS GO WRONG HAS
THOUGHT OF SOMEONE
TO BLAME IT ON.

ROBERT BLOCH

The Irish love to be loved,
except by each other.

DAVID KENNY

BETTER FIFTY ENEMIES OUTSIDE THE HOUSE THAN ONE WITHIN.

IRISH PROVERB

Murder is always a mistake. One should never do anything that one cannot talk about after dinner.

OSCAR WILDE

WHEN IRISH EYES ARE SMILING, WATCH YOUR STEP.

GERALD KERSH

Who gossips with you will gossip of you.

IRISH PROVERB

PUT AN IRISHMAN ON THE SPIT AND YOU CAN ALWAYS GET ANOTHER IRISHMAN TO TURN HIM.

GEORGE BERNARD SHAW

WELL
PENNED

The difference between literature and journalism is that journalism is unreadable and literature is unread.

OSCAR WILDE

ONE DAY YOU GET SOME SILVER, AND THE NEXT DAY YOU JUST GET ROCK.

EAVAN BOLAND ON WRITING POETRY

The Irish love words and
use as many of them in
a sentence as possible.

ANNE McCAFFREY

IRELAND IS RICH IN
LITERATURE THAT
UNDERSTANDS A SOUL'S
YEARNINGS, AND DANCING
THAT UNDERSTANDS
A HAPPY HEART.

MARGARET JACKSON

I always start writing with a clean
piece of paper and a dirty mind.

PATRICK DENNIS

WRITING IS LEARNING
TO SAY NOTHING, MORE
CLEVERLY EACH DAY.

WILLIAM ALLINGHAM

Anybody can write a three-volume
novel. It merely requires a complete
ignorance of both life and literature.

OSCAR WILDE

I HAVE MY FAULTS,
BUT CHANGING MY TUNE
IS NOT ONE OF THEM.

SAMUEL BECKETT

I often quote myself.
It adds spice to my conversation.

GEORGE BERNARD SHAW

AN AUTHOR'S FIRST DUTY IS
TO LET DOWN HIS COUNTRY.

BRENDAN BEHAN

The sound of Irish seems to be
lodged in the sub-conscious
mind of our people.

KATE FENNELL

WHEN I DIE I WANT TO
DECOMPOSE IN A BARREL
OF PORTER AND HAVE IT
SERVED... IN DUBLIN.

J. P. DONLEAVY

Of our conflicts with others we
make rhetoric; of our conflicts
with ourselves we make poetry.

W. B. YEATS

I WAS BORN ON A
STORM-SWEPT ROCK
AND HATE THE
SOFT GROWTH OF
SUN-BAKED LANDS.

LIAM O'FLAHERTY

Being Irish, I always had
this love of words.

KENNETH BRANAGH

I THINK THERE'S
SOMETHING ABOUT THE
IRISH EXPERIENCE – THAT
WE HAD TO HAVE A SENSE
OF HUMOUR OR DIE.

FRANK McCOURT

*I'm an old snail
leaving a constant
trail of slime,*

*and sometimes
it glistens.*

JOHN BANVILLE ON WRITING

James Joyce was a true artist
from his head to his crotch.

ALEC GUINNESS

OUR IRISH BLUNDERS
ARE NEVER BLUNDERS
OF THE HEART.

MARIA EDGEWORTH

Memoirs are a well-known
form of fiction.

FRANK HARRIS

A SCHOLAR'S INK LASTS LONGER THAN A MARTYR'S BLOOD.

IRISH PROVERB

Shakespeare said pretty well everything and what he left out, James Joyce, with a nudge from meself, put in.

BRENDAN BEHAN

RAGS TO
RICHES

THE ONLY THING THAT CAN CONSOLE ONE FOR BEING POOR IS EXTRAVAGANCE.

OSCAR WILDE

To be clever enough to get a great deal of money, one must be stupid enough to want it.

GEORGE BERNARD SHAW

MONEY CAN'T BUY YOU HAPPINESS BUT IT DOES BRING YOU A MORE PLEASANT FORM OF MISERY.

SPIKE MILLIGAN

MONEY CANNOT BUY
HAPPINESS, BUT IT'S
MORE COMFORTABLE
TO CRY IN A MERCEDES
THAN ON A BICYCLE.

Irish proverb

A MAN'S RESPECT FOR LAW
AND ORDER EXISTS IN
PRECISE RELATIONSHIP TO
THE SIZE OF HIS PAYCHECK.

ADAM CLAYTON

If anyone broke into our house,
they'd leave a donation.

FRANK CARSON

TEA IS THE CHAMPAGNE
OF THE POOR.

HUGH LEONARD

POOR NATIONS ARE
HUNGRY, AND RICH
NATIONS ARE PROUD; AND
PRIDE AND HUNGER WILL
EVER BE AT VARIANCE.

JONATHAN SWIFT

*A heavy purse
makes a light heart.*

IRISH PROVERB

Money does not make you
happy but it quiets the nerves.

SEÁN O'CASEY

WITH A GROUP OF BANKERS
I ALWAYS HAD THE FEELING
THAT SUCCESS WAS MEASURED
BY THE EXTENT ONE
GAVE NOTHING AWAY.

FRANCIS AUNGIER

The best way to keep loyalty
in a man's heart is to keep
money in his purse.

IRISH PROVERB

VERY FEW PEOPLE CAN
AFFORD TO BE POOR.

GEORGE BERNARD SHAW

You might be poor, your shoes
might be broken, but your
mind is a palace.

FRANK McCOURT

NOTHING IS MORE EXPENSIVE
THAN A GIRL WHO'S FREE
FOR THE EVENING.

HAL ROACH

Law grinds the poor, and
rich men rule the law.

OLIVER GOLDSMITH

TIME
GONE BY

WE LOVE THE 'STORY' PART OF
THE WORD 'HISTORY', AND
WE LOVE IT TRIMMED OUT
WITH COLOUR AND DRAMA.

FRANK DELANEY

One of the good things about
modern Ireland is that you don't
have to hang around in libraries
anymore to get warm.

RODDY DOYLE

THE IRELAND I NOW INHABIT
IS ONE THAT THESE IRISH
CONTEMPORARIES HAVE
HELPED TO IMAGINE.

SEAMUS HEANEY

Every St Patrick's Day every Irishman goes out to find another Irishman to make a speech to.

SHANE LESLIE

PROGRESS MEANS GETTING NEARER TO THE PLACE YOU WANT TO BE.

C. S. LEWIS

I was elected by the women of Ireland, who instead of rocking the cradle, rocked the system.

MARY ROBINSON

A GOOD STORYTELLER NEVER LETS THE FACTS GET IN THE WAY.

Dave Allen

THE IRISH, AND I'M GUILTY
OF THIS, THINK THEY
INVENTED EVERYTHING.

BONO

History… is a nightmare from
which I am trying to awake.

JAMES JOYCE, *ULYSSES*

IRELAND… WAS A NINETEENTH
CENTURY SOCIETY UP TO
ABOUT 1970 AND THEN
IT ALMOST BYPASSED THE
TWENTIETH CENTURY.

JOHN McGAHERN

You can never plan
the future by the past.

EDMUND BURKE

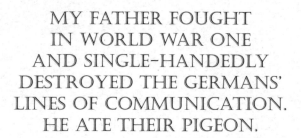

MY FATHER FOUGHT
IN WORLD WAR ONE
AND SINGLE-HANDEDLY
DESTROYED THE GERMANS'
LINES OF COMMUNICATION.
HE ATE THEIR PIGEON.

FRANK CARSON

St Patrick's Day is named
for St Patrick, the first guy
to feed Guinness to a snake.

CONAN O'BRIEN

THERE CAN BE NO TRADITION
WITHOUT INNOVATION.

EARLE HITCHNER

IRISH
LOGIC

From now on it's the start
of a new beginning.

DON GIVENS

I MAY NOT BE KNOWN
OUTSIDE IRELAND BUT I'M
WORLD-FAMOUS IN DUBLIN.

BUTCH MOORE

There's nothing so bad
that couldn't be worse.

IRISH PROVERB

'I WILL, YEAH,' CORKONIANS
SAY WHEN THEY MEAN 'NEVER'.

DAVID MONAGAN

If you have the words, there's always
a chance that you'll find the way.

SEAMUS HEANEY

I WOULDN'T MIND THE RAIN
IF IT WASN'T FOR THE WET.

JIM SHANAHAN

If my father was alive to see the modern world, he'd turn in his grave.

MICHAEL O'DOHERTY

THE THING TO PREVENT WHAT'S PAST IS TO PUT A STOP TO IT BEFORE IT HAPPENS.

BOYLE ROCHE

Rainbows aren't optical illusions. They only look like them.

JIMEOIN

CLOSED ON ACCOUNT
OF RE-OPENING

SIGN ON A SHOP WINDOW, CORK

Here's to women's kisses,
And to whiskey, amber-clear;
Not as sweet as a woman's kiss,
But a darn sight more sincere.

IRISH PROVERB

*I believe in
the discipline
of silence,
and could talk
for hours
about it.*

GEORGE
BERNARD
SHAW

HAPPY ARE THE PARENTS WHO HAVE NO CHILDREN.

BOYLE ROCHE

My father discovered a cure for amnesia but he forgot what it was.

NOEL PURCELL

THE ONLY THING THAT HAS TO BE FINISHED BY NEXT FRIDAY IS NEXT THURSDAY.

MAUREEN POTTER

HOME
TRUTHS

At home in Ireland, there's a habit of avoidance, an ironical attitude towards the authority figure.

SEAMUS HEANEY

IRELAND IS AMERICA'S 52ND STATE.

NOËL BROWNE

Only the Irish working class remains as the incorruptible inheritors of the fight for freedom in Ireland.

JAMES CONNOLLY

DUBLIN UNIVERSITY CONTAINS THE CREAM OF IRELAND: RICH AND THICK.

SAMUEL BECKETT

Perhaps 'fiddler on the hoof' might be a more appropriate name for Irish racing.

BRENDAN McGAHON

I WAS BORN IRISH AND HAVE CONTINUED TO BE SO ALL MY LIFE.

COLONEL SAUNDERSON

I think of the bog as a feminine goddess-ridden ground, rather like the territory of Ireland itself.

SEAMUS HEANEY

IF YOU DON'T DRINK OR
SNORT COKE OR SLEEP WITH
COLIN FARRELL, THERE'S
NOTHING TO DO IN DUBLIN.

SINÉAD O'CONNOR

The term 'Irish Secret Service'
is as big a contradiction as
'British Intelligence'.

DAVID NORRIS

BEING A WOMAN IS LIKE BEING
IRISH... EVERYONE SAYS YOU'RE
IMPORTANT AND NICE, BUT
YOU TAKE SECOND PLACE.

IRIS MURDOCH

Ireland is the old sow
that eats her farrow.

JAMES JOYCE

IF YOU SUCCEED IN IRELAND
IT'S LIKE, 'WHO DO YOU
THINK YOU ARE?
I KNEW YOU WERE NOTHING.'

BOB GELDOF

Moderation, we find, is an extremely
difficult thing to get in this country.

FLANN O'BRIEN

PARTING
SHOTS

Because they were extinguished looking as distinct from distinguished looking, I divined that they were journalists.

CON HOULIHAN

A CRITIC IS A PERSON WHO WILL SLIT THE THROAT OF A SKYLARK TO SEE WHAT MAKES IT SING.

J. M. SYNGE

*May your spade
never dig,
may your sow
never pig.*

IRISH PROVERB

I can't stand media people
interviewing each other.
It reminds me of ingrown toenails.

BRENDAN O'REGAN

IF YOU HAD A BRAIN CELL,
IT WOULD DIE OF LONELINESS.

JOHN O'DWYER

She has an ego
like a raging tooth.

W. B. YEATS

IF I SAY THAT HE'S EXTREMELY
STUPID, I DON'T MEAN THAT
IN ANY DEROGATORY SENSE.

BRENDAN O'CARROLL

Your features don't seem to
know the value of teamwork.

GENE FITZPATRICK

MY WIFE IS THE SORT
OF WOMAN WHO GIVES
NECROPHILIA A BAD NAME.

PATRICK MURRAY

She had all the characteristics
of a poker, with the exception
of its occasional warmth.

DANIEL O'DONNELL

NORTHERN IRELAND IS THE
WORLD'S BEST-KEPT SECRET
BOTH IN THE CHARACTER OF
ITS PEOPLE AND ITS SCENERY.

LIAM NEESON

I LOVED HER SO MUCH
I NAMED MY FIRST
ULCER AFTER HER.

Dusty Young

I have met a lot of
hardboiled eggs in
my time, but you're
twenty minutes.

OSCAR WILDE

Every great European race
has sent its stream to the
river of the Irish mind.

THOMAS DAVIS

YOU HAVE A FACE THAT
WOULD DRIVE RATS
FROM A BARN.

IRISH PROVERB

If you expect a kick in
the balls and you get a slap
in the face, it's a victory.

ARDAL O'HANLON

May his pipe never smoke,
may his teapot be broke
And to add to the joke, may
his kettle ne'er boil;
May he keep to the bed till
the hour that he's dead,
May he always be fed on
hogwash and boiled oil.
May he swell with the gout,
may his grinders fall out,
May he roll, howl and shout
with the horrid toothache;
May the temples wear horns,
and the toes many corns,
Of the monster that murdered
Nell Flaherty's drake.

**IRISH CURSE FROM 'NELL FLAHERTY'S DRAKE'
(IRISH FOLK SONG)**

THERE IS NO HERESY OR
NO PHILOSOPHY WHICH
IS SO ABHORRENT TO THE
CHURCH AS A HUMAN BEING.

JAMES JOYCE

May the cat eat you
and the devil eat the cat.

IRISH PROVERB

HE HASN'T A SINGLE
REDEEMING VICE.

OSCAR WILDE

FOR A YOUNG GIRL TO BE
NAMED 'WHOLESOME' IS
PERHAPS THE DEADLIEST
INSULT OF ALL.

CAITLIN THOMAS

Never hit an Irishman
when he's down.
He might get up again.

SEAMUS O'LEARY

MAY YOU DIE IN BED
AT NINETY-FIVE YEARS,
SHOT BY A JEALOUS
HUSBAND (OR WIFE).

IRISH TOAST

He'd be out of his depth
on a wet pavement.

JOE O'SHEA

MAY ALL THE GOATS IN
GOREY CHASE YOU TO HELL.

IRISH CURSE

YOU'RE AS THICK
AS MANURE BUT ONLY
HALF AS USEFUL.

Irish proverb

May you be afflicted with the itch
but have no nails to scratch with!

IRISH CURSE

SMACK TALK? THIS IS AN
AMERICAN TERM THAT MAKES
ME LAUGH. I SIMPLY SPEAK THE
TRUTH. I'M AN IRISH MAN.

CONOR McGREGOR

I never forget an Irish face, but in your case I'll make an exception.

ANONYMOUS

NO, THAT SKIRT DOESN'T MAKE YOU LOOK FATTER. HOW COULD IT?

MAUREEN POTTER

Donncha Ó Dúlaing has his place. It's a small jail in Guatemala.

DERMOT MORGAN

Why don't you write books people can read?

NORA BARNACLE TO HER HUSBAND JAMES JOYCE

WHO KNOWS WHAT
HELLISH FUTURE LIES
AHEAD? ACTUALLY I DO,
I'VE SEEN THE REHEARSALS.

**TERRY WOGAN, INTRODUCING
THE 2007 *EUROVISION SONG CONTEST***

There are two ways of disliking
poetry; one way is to dislike it,
the other is to read Pope.

OSCAR WILDE

YOU'RE AS SHARP
AS A BEACHBALL.

IRISH PROVERB

IN THE HUMAN RACE TODAY, YOU CAME LAST.

Spike Milligan

IRISH
AND PROUD OF IT

EILEEN FITZGERALD

IRISH AND PROUD OF IT

Eileen Fitzgerald

Hardback
£5.99
978-1-84953-522-9

Dear Erin, how sweetly
thy green bosom rises!
An emerald set in the
ring of the sea.

John Philpot Curran

Celebrate your roots and discover in this miscellany of facts and quotes a cornucopia of Ireland's treasures and history. It's enough to make any Irish person proud.

THE LITTLE
BOOK OF
IRISH
JOKES

Cormac O'Brien

THE LITTLE BOOK OF IRISH JOKES

Cormac O'Brien

Paperback
£5.99
978-1-84953-953-1

'What would you be
if you weren't Irish?'
asked the barman.

Pat replied, 'Ashamed!'

There are two types of people in this world: the Irish, and those who wish they were. But wherever you're from, this little book is packed with grand gags and celtic wisecracks that will give you the gift of the gab and a belly full of laughs.

If you're interested in finding out more
about our books, find us on Facebook
at Summersdale Publishers and
follow us on Twitter at @Summersdale.

www.summersdale.com